How to Create
PICTURE
BOOKS
FOR KIDS

DONIA YOUSSEF

www.themonster-series.com

ISBN: 978-1-7398724-4-1 (Paperback)
ISBN: 978-1-7398724-5-8 (Hardcover)

Cover illustrated by Ravi Shankar
Book designed by Nonon Tech & Design

Dedicated to
my daughters Aaliyah and Tiana ♥

TABLE OF CONTENTS

CHAPTER 1

INTRODUCTION

I t might be tempting to think that writing a children's picture book is easier than writing a full-length novel. However, a picture book requires all the same major storytelling elements that a novel does — such as well-drawn characters and an intriguing plot — just in a much smaller space.

The good news is that if you can achieve these things (with engaging illustrations to boot!), you'll be poised to inspire the imaginations of young readers, who are always looking to welcome their next beloved picture book into their library.

There is a booming children's picture book market, and for good reason. Writing your own children's book can be a rewarding experience and until recently, creating e-book versions of children's picture books was something publishers reserved for their best-selling authors and illustrators. The truth is, anyone can sit down and dash out a children's book, and with a little help and guidance, yours can be good enough to earn the attention of thousands of children. And nothing beats the feeling of holding your printed book in your hands and reading it to a child for the first time.

One helpful tip to help you on this journey is to know that successful picture books are the ones that strike the right balance between appealing to two different audiences: while a picture book is intended for children, it's ultimately the parents who decide whether to buy it — or to read it aloud. (That being said, appealing to and entertaining adults shouldn't take priority over the children you're writing your children's picture book for.)

In this course, I will be providing answers to questions like

✎ HOW DO I WRITE IT?

You probably have an idea for a children's book, but you might struggle to get it on the page. It's tough to know how to tell the story so children will really enjoy it.

✎ IS IT ANY GOOD?

After writing your children's book, you're not sure how to make it better. Sure, kids will sit through it one time — but will they clamour to hear it a second time?

✎ HOW DO I PUBLISH?

You have your book, but you don't know how to write a query letter, hire an illustrator, approach an agent, or send your book to publishers. It's a very steep learning curve.

Having worked with a lot of frustrated writers who spent months and even years trying to write and publish their children's picture book,

I believe I can help you on your journey to creating your first picture book. Let me be your guide and radically speed up the process. I've saved thousands of writers from heartache.

You'll have in depth insight into:
- How to generate a concept that works
- How to create a main character that children love
- How to write the right length
- How to use illustrations that speaks to children
- How to structure the plot
- How to work with an illustrator
- How to revise
- How to publish

Are you eager to tackle this task? Let us begin!

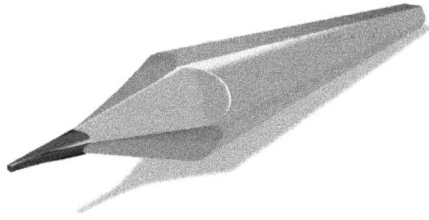

CHAPTER 2

WHAT IS
A PICTURE BOOK - TYPES

A picture book is a story intended for the youngest of readers, in which the illustrations and the text work together to tell the story. Picture books are usually read to children, not by children.

They are meant for children who are not yet able to read, and help them develop a sense of storytelling, plot, and language recognition. Picture books have illustrations on every page because looking at art helps with story comprehension and understanding that words have meaning.

The illustrations also help children contextualize text by giving visual cues to the meaning of the words on a page. In addition, picture book illustrations strengthen a child's observation skills, as there is often more happening in the art than stated in the text. But understanding the definition of a picture book is not the same as understanding essential elements that make a great picture book: picture book word count, age range, and page count to name a few. So, let's take a look at some varieties of picture books!

✎ BOARD BOOKS

These are usually made for new-born babies to around 2 years old. They have thick paperboard pages to combat wear and tear from baby hands and mouths. There may be more interactive elements to these books such as cloth, noise, or popups to engage a baby or allow the reader to make the story more exciting. Parents and caregivers love board books because they are the perfect guides for a child's first steps in social emotional learning, self-care, and manners.

✎ CONCEPT BOOKS

This type of picture book made to explain or introduce an idea or activity. This includes the alphabet, counting, colours, times, and shapes. Some can be as simple as "A is for Apple." Others are more complex like the "Miss Bindergarten" series, where each sentence uses a letter of the alphabet to tell a Kindergarten story.

✎ EARLY READERS

These are designed to have more of a structure similar to a chapter book but uses a more limited vocabulary. The text blocks are bigger and the included images function more as illustrations than as essential elements in the story. Some representative Easy Reader imprints are I Can Read, Ready to Read, and Easy-to-Read.

✏ WORDLESS

A story made up of only pictures! A child can create their own story through the illustrations, especially when they are at a pre-literacy age. Making up stories to go with the pictures is a perfect activity to engage young minds.

✏ TRANSITION BOOKS

This type of picture book features fewer images and usually they are in black and white. Just as their name suggests, they are the bridge for a reader to begin reading chapter books.

✏ NARRATIVE NONFICTION

These tells a nonfiction story in a picture format that can help more reluctant young readers become interested and provide them fun facts through visual storytelling.

Picture books also come in a wide range of genres and feature immersive storylines, engaging content, beautiful illustrations, and makes reading fun for young readers! We will be getting into the practicalities of creating a successful picture book.

✏ FICTION PICTURE BOOKS

Fiction means you're making up a story. This is the most common kind of picture book, and when it comes to what it can be about, the sky's the limit. There is no reason you can't write about whatever makes you—or your children—happy.

But again, keep in mind your target audience. Children of this age are still learning about the world, so picture books, no matter how serious or whimsical, tend to present situations and characters young children can understand and relate to.

Therefore, subjects such as farm, bedtime, friendship, and ABC are perennially popular. One of the first things we teach our kids is what sounds animals make, so this is a subject matter they are familiar with and can relate to. A book about a class test, on the other hand, won't be something a four-year-old who has never been in school can understand.

CHAPTER 3

WHAT IS A PICTURE BOOK: PRACTICALITIES

You have this great idea to create a picture book but how do you start? The first thing you need to figure out is what exactly does it entail? What are the practicalities involved? Let's take this one at a time:

✎ PICTURE BOOK WORD COUNT

Traditional guidance says picture book word count should not exceed 1,000 words. And, in fact, this is the cap that many agents put on manuscripts. If your book is longer than 1,000 words, they won't even review it. In reality, the sweet spot is closer to 500-700 words.

Keep in mind when writing your book that picture books are meant to be read aloud. When picture book word count exceeds 1,000 words, books tend to become cumbersome, often taking too long to read. If you are a parent, think about those books you read to your kids at night. How often have you said, "Not that one? It's too long." No matter how great your story is, if a parent feels like it's too long, they won't want to read it. And remember, at the end of the day, they are the ones purchasing the books.

✎ PICTURE BOOK SIZES

Picture books can truly be any size you want. They can be square, portrait, or landscape.

As you move toward figuring out trim size, just remember that a picture book is meant to be read aloud. Whether that is two people holding it across their laps or a someone showing it off from the front of a classroom or library, the book needs to be seen. If you go too small, you run the risk of not making it sharable.

✎ SHOULD A PICTURE BOOK BE WRITTEN IN PAST TENSE OR PRESENT TENSE?

Most picture books are written in past tense. That is because they skip around in time. Present tense works well in books for older readers because we can get inside a narrator's head and find out what we missed. But with picture books, that's not usually an option. Present tense is great if the entire story is told without any time lags, but if you are jumping around at all, it will likely read better in past tense.

✎ PICTURE BOOK PAGE COUNT

Generally speaking, picture books are 32 pages long, although they can also be 24, 40, or 48 pages. If you plan to print using an offset printer, it's imperative that you stick to one of these page counts. If you plan to print on demand, page count is up to you (although sticking to generally accepted norms is never a bad idea.)

✏ PICTURE BOOK LENGTH

Picture books are traditionally 32 pages. The way those pages are set up typically follows a particular order and particular guidelines.

✏ PICTURE BOOK FRONT COVER

Your book cover should list your title (ideally in the top third of the book) as well as the author and illustrator name.

Standard practice is to cite the author simply by name, while citing the illustrator as "Illustrated by"

✏ PICTURE BOOK SPINE

The spine of your book is the part that faces out when a book is on the shelf. It should feature 3 elements, running from top to bottom:

Author/illustrator last name

Title

Company or imprint name (larger publishing companies are broken into several divisions, each with their own unique acquisition list and personality. Each section is called an imprint.)

Spine text should be set with the bottom of the letters facing the back cover.

✏ PICTURE BOOK BACK COVER

The back cover of a book should contain your book description (also called cover copy or book blurb). If you are not including a dust jacket, you may also want to include an author bio on the back cover, as well as your price.

With all these pieces in place, you should have idea about what it takes to create a great picture book. Just remember, always keep one question in mind above all others: WHO IS MY BOOK FOR?

CHAPTER 4

THE INITIAL IDEA

Now that you know the practicalities involved, it's time to come up with a great book! Of course, it's not always easy. For some authors, after that debut book, it's hard to come up with another story idea. At least, it's hard to generate story ideas that work—that are worth writing about. And for an author who wants to build a business around their children's books, that can be a problem. Waiting too long to publish the next book can mean readers forget about you. The good news is, you're not alone. Even the most experienced children's book authors sometimes struggle to come up with their next book idea. The difference is, they have strategies in place to generate story ideas. Let's look into ways to bring about these ideas!

1. LISTEN TO CHILDREN

When it comes to story ideas for children's books, there's no one better you can take advice from than a child. Why? Because they have such wild imaginations! Story generation just comes naturally to them. From doctors who treat monkey farts to flying superheroes who shoot water from their feet, a child's imagination is never at rest. Kids are always making up games, too. One minute they are doctors, the next they are going to the moon or have turned into pirates. Pay attention to their play patterns and see how you can extend them into your own story ideas. Listen to what comes out of their mouths and see where you can draw inspiration. What theme do they most often return to? What excites them? What excites you? As you listen to children around you playing and talking, see if anything particularly strikes you as an idea for a new book idea.

Remember, children's books are for children. They are the audience you need to appeal to. So, use what already appeals to them as a jumping off point to come up with new book ideas.

2. JOURNAL YOUR CHILDHOOD EXPERIENCES

Sit down with a notebook and start writing down book ideas. Don't worry about what they are, just get whatever comes into your head onto paper. Focus on your own experiences as a child. What is the funnies thing that ever happened to you? The saddest? The silliest? When were you most proud? If asked for a childhood memory, what sticks out the most? A moment with a parent or grandparent? A moment at school?

All these experiences provide fodder for book ideas, so dig into them and see what resonates. And don't forget to think about your own childhood emotions. How did certain situations make you feel? Emotion is a strong part of children's books, so if you can tap into a moment in your own childhood that carries with it a strong emotion, you may find a good story angle!

3.   BRAINSTORM CHARACTER AND SETTING IDEAS

On a piece of paper, try writing down a list of characters, settings, and plots. Then mix and match and see what you come up with. Once you have your setting, try turning it upside down. Is there one big change you could make that would change the entire landscape of your story? Is the whole world backward? Or upside down? You might find a funny (or sentimental) book idea hiding in there that wouldn't have come to you if the who, what, and where hadn't been randomly thrown together.

4.   KEEP AN IDEAS JOURNAL

We've all had a great story idea and then forgotten it. Sometimes it's a dream we forget within minutes of waking up, or an idea in the shower. Maybe watching a child's dance recital. Wherever your ideas come from, keep a notebook close by to write down any idea that comes to you (or if you're so inclined, create a list on your phone.) Wherever that place is, make it a dedicated story list. By always keeping your story ideas in the same place, you'll know where to go to find them when you're ready.

5.   WRITING PROMPTS

A writing prompt offers up no more than the first few words of a story. It's a chance to get your head spinning. And they're easy to find. A quick internet search will reveal hundreds. So why not use them as a jumping off point for your book idea? You don't have to keep the opening lines, but they might help you find the story idea you've been looking for!

✎ 6. TRY A DIFFERENT POINT OF VIEW

Have you written a story, but it doesn't feel right? Maybe your protagonist shouldn't be your protagonist. What would happen if you told the story from a different point of view? Try retelling it from every character's perspective. Does one feel better than another? If nothing else, you'll learn more about your characters, which will result in richer storytelling.

✎ 7. START AT THE END OF A STORY

Sometimes starting a story can be challenging. But ending one is fun. It's a resolution. So, start there. Write how your story ends. Then back up and figure out what had to happen in order for your characters to reach that resolution!

CHAPTER 5

TRADITIONAL TALES AS INSPIRATION

It is well known that writers are some of the most creative people ever, but not everything they write is original. It's not that we deliberately copy anyone else's work, but we do very often draw ideas, themes, patterns, storylines, and even character types from many different sources. Everything we've ever read, heard, and seen is part of our mental landscape, spinning around in our imaginations, getting remixed, influencing creative process, and showing up in interesting ways in our final products.

Important elements in this mix are three sources that are part of the shared heritage of Western culture and civilization: myths, traditional stories, and religious works, especially the Bible. In this lesson, we're going to investigate how to make use of traditional tales as an inspiration for your picture book.

WHY ARE TRADITIONAL TALES IMPORTANT?

Traditional tales are prominent stories in a culture that are passed down between generations and retold countless times. Often the term is used interchangeably with fairy stories and fairy tales.

Traditional tales are different from children's fables which illustrate a moral lesson. This makes it easy to use as ideas in picture books and capture the attention of kids as well as serve as a way to teach them exemplary values.

What's more? Children enjoy Storytime at school and at home, so these memorable characters are ideal for English learning aids. These well-loved stories were made for passing down and retelling many times and adapting for different times in human history. You can make use of these well-known stories to form ideas.

TIPS TO USE:

▲ Read lots of traditional tales.

▲ You could watch the film adaptations too, and then look back over the traditional stories to compare and see if the character on screen is how you would like children to picture them from the book.

▲ Discuss the story and the characters with those you trust. Is it easy to identify the heroes and villains? What did they think of the characters? Who was their favourite?

▲ Asking lots of questions will help to develop any idea forming in your mind, as they will start to relate to the characters and be able to see who has which role within the story and why.

▲ Open ended questions are best, so that you have to think back to certain parts of the story, for example 'What was the second little pigs house made of?' or 'What made Sleeping Beauty fall asleep?'.

▲ Other things to discuss to help you think more deeply about the characters could be asking how you think certain characters would have felt, and what you think they could have done differently. For example, 'do you think Goldilocks felt bad about stealing the little bears porridge?'.

▲ You can draft your story structure and write down your story gradually, by folding a piece of paper into three. Each section is the beginning, middle and end, and you can plan out your story using the boxes to show what will happen and at what stage.

CHAPTER 6

CHARACTERS: HUMANS, ANIMALS, FAIRIES – AND PENCILS!

W riting characters can be either the most fun or the most tedious aspect of creating your story. Sometimes characters can come to us like a dream—you can hear them talking if you close your eyes and they are just so vivid that you can imagine them being a real person. Other times ... well, let's just say we know when we're taking any old, blank canvas along for a joy ride in place of a well-thought-out character.

Remember that characters drive plots. It's important that other children like and empathise with the characters you create. They must care about what happens next because of them.

Your readers want to know how they will handle difficult situations. They have to understand them and their personality traits, both the negative and the positive. As writers we must get our readers to empathise with our creations and to care if they succeed or fail. If the main characters do not seem real in our imaginations, or in the settings we choose, children will lose interest in them.

Too many characters confuse young readers. As children's books become longer and your audience older, there is room for more characters and more in-depth character development.

Four Things To Remember

1. You do not have to describe characters in picture books. Characters are shown in illustrations. You can't afford to include descriptions with a limited word count. Try to include only what is necessary for the story to make sense.

2. The reader needs to think of your characters as real people. Take interesting bits and pieces from people you know, mix them up, and create characters who are unique.

3. Characters act and speak. Actions show personality. What they do and how they react depends on their background, their experiences, and their personality type. The best characters act consistently.

4. Every character needs a reason to feature in your book. What do your characters want? What motivates them? Why do they want it? Young readers must be able to relate to your characters.

Let's talk about the five fundamental elements you should know inside and out about your picture-book characters

✏ 1. NAME

Names should be word pictures of the character. What kind of character might you name Amanda, which comes from Latin and means "worthy of love"? Would you name a happy-go-lucky child Miriam, which has origins in Hebrew and means "sea of sorrow, or bitterness"?

What type of character might have a hard-sounding name like Curt? What personality might a boy need in order to be named Misha, with its soft sounds? Or should you defy expectations and name the gentle character Curt and the tough guy Misha? Someone working on a story about dogs for instance, them naming a dalmatian Blaze and a chihuahua Thimble… do you see the angle here?

While discussing names, here's the fastest way to get your story noticed by an editor for the wrong reasons: giving your characters alliterative names. What you might not realize is that naming characters like Sammy Skunk and Billy Beaver shouts "cute" and "lack of respect for the child listener" and makes it easy for the editor to drop your story in the form-rejection-letter pile or not even bother with a response.

A good rule of thumb is to simply call the animals what they are (e.g., Bear, Mouse, Duck, Frog, and Mole). Or give the animal a single human name like. Also, try not to give characters names that might confuse the child listener. Names that are too similar like Matthew and Martin probably belong in separate stories. The name of your character will usually indicate the sex of the child unless you are trying to keep this ambiguous. Susan and Sally are obviously girls' names. Justin and Jacob are boys' names.

Giving your character a nickname is fine, but if you want it to be easy to remember and enrich your characterization, you should give a short explanation of its origin.

2. BIRTHDATE AND AGE

The birthdate helps place your story in a historical period. A five-year-old child born in 1700 will be unlike a five-year-old child born in 2018. And probably named differently, too. Zebadiah is rarely the name of a child born in 2018. If you write about a child born in the mid-1700s, you can use words like carriage, blacksmith, and hornbook—words you wouldn't choose if your character were born today.

How old is your character, and in what ways does age influence his behaviour? A two-year-old behaves unlike a four-year-old or an eight-year-old. Does your character act his age? Does he speak in baby talk? Maybe he tries to act tough like his big brother. Perhaps the other characters assume he is older or younger than he really is.

3. APPEARANCE

If your character is an animal, state that. It is important to know. It's a good idea to keep a photograph from family snapshots or clippings from magazines and newspapers that resembles your character. Note that the illustrator may paint a character far removed from what you imagine. However, having a picture in your mind, whether it matches the illustrator's, makes for strong writing.

Think about whether your character spends lots of time on appearance or if such concerns are of little consequence to him. Is he generally pleased with how he looks? Is he neat or sloppy? What kind of clothes might he wear? Health might be important here, too. Maybe your character exercises a lot or gets sick often.

✎ 4. RELATIONSHIPS

Start first with family, especially if they are important in the story. Who are the parents, siblings, and extended family? It's not enough to just give names here. Let the reader know about their personalities and interactions.

What problems does your main character have with them? Is the family from a foreign country? If so, explain any activities or beliefs that are unique to their culture and whether they like their new home. Family income may be relevant if it affects your main character. The frequency with which he sees his parents could be a factor in their relationship. What about friends? Neighbours? Teachers? We might need to know how your main character feels about them, too.

✎ 5. PERSONALITY

I've saved the most important area to focus on for last. Look at picture books you love and think about the characters. How would you define Sophie's personality in Sophie's Squash? What about Ralph in Ralph Tells a Story by Abby Hanlon? Are they similar? Differentiating between characters in published books will help you better define your own characters.

List your character's strengths and weaknesses, attitudes, fears, obsessions, special talents, and hobbies. Does your character have a favourite saying like "Go for it!" or a habit of tapping her fingers when she is bored? Try writing yourself a letter from your character about what happens in the story—it will help you hear her voice directly.

CHAPTER 7

BADDIES

An awesome villain can really make a great children's book. Oh sure, it's great to have a hero who models virtue and courage, but it's the villains who are often the most interesting and memorable characters.

You may have heard the saying "a story is only as good as its characters." This statement is only half true. A story is only as good as its baddies; therefore, you can't have a good story without an antagonist.

While villains can be virtually anything – an element, monster, animal, or person – it is important to give them defining features, a motivation (no matter how trivial) that prevents the main character from achieving their goals, a way to be defeated, and, depending on the story, a backstory on why they became villains.

The types of villains in picture books are often not your standard looking villain. Why? Because we are telling a story to kids, about kids, and for kids. This means we must show what is villainous to them.

Not villains that dominate the whole world but things that dominate a child's world. We are mini sizing the bad guys into things children can relate to. Things kids deal with daily; those are a child's worst nightmares.

✎ YOUR ANTAGONIST'S MOTIVATION

Giving your antagonist a motivation will really make your story stand out and make your readers love to hate your antagonist. If you are going for the classic villain or an opposing character type, make sure their motivations are strong.

Depending on the type of antagonist your character is, you can decide how explicit you want their reasoning to be.

Let's look at the Other Mother from Coraline, for instance. She is an example of a classic villain. What makes her an amazing antagonist is the fact she comes off as a caring mother at first that wants to make Coraline happy. However, the readers see the change in the middle of the book when she is revealed to be a beldam (witch) that feeds off the souls of children.

Her character motivation is terrifying, yet that's what makes her a compelling character.

Look at Lisette from Bewitching. She's the opposing character antagonist whose motivation for essentially ruining Emma's life is jealousy. She is jealous that Emma still has her mom, has a good relationship with her dad, didn't have to grow up poor, and is beautiful. Throughout the story, Lisette does everything in her power to ensure that Emma is miserable by making sure she stays unpopular, steals her boyfriend, and is always at Emma's father's side.

Lisette's motivation is what made that story so interesting and made us root for Emma.

In a way, the inanimate force antagonists can have motivations, too. While their motivations are more implied to readers, they still can become fascinating villains.

✎ YOUR ANTAGONIST'S DEFINING FEATURES

A common complaint amongst readers is how some stories' antagonists' motivations do not make any sense or are weak. To ensure that doesn't happen, deciding what defines your chosen antagonist as an obstacle will help majorly with their motivation.

First, think about what aspects about them make them an antagonist. Many writers give their antagonists tragic backstories to help define them.

Let's look at Luke from Percy Jackson and the Olympians series. He is a classic villain whose tragic backstory is that the Oracle of Delphi cursed his mother with getting glimpses of the future. As a result, his mother went crazy. She abused and neglected Luke as a result.

Since Luke was the son of Hermes, he hardly heard from his dad and was constantly chased by monsters up until he found refuge at Camp Half-Blood – a summer camp for demigods. On his way to Camp Half-Blood, he watched his best friend Thalia get killed by monsters. The final straw was when he went on a quest to steal a golden apple when he got attacked by a dragon and failed his quest.

This backstory became the catalyst for him to join the titan Kronos's forces, who offered him a permanent home, support, and to become the leader of his army.

This story defines Luke's character as it shows that he came from a broken home, went through numerous traumatic experiences, and nobody seemed to care about him. When Kronos visited Luke in a dream inviting him to join him and providing him that support and praise, he desperately craved, readers could understand why Luke did not hesitate to accept the titan's offer.

Outside of a tragic backstory, there are other ways of defining an antagonist. If you have a classic villain or an opposing villain who has a more ominous presence in the story, giving them intimidating features or crude behaviours helps with that as well.

Look at Voldemort from Harry Potter. While in the Half-Blood Prince we understand why Voldemort became a villain, there are other aspects that make him a memorable antagonist.

For starters, his unbelievable power. He was able to cheat death because he split his soul seven times and placed them in objects called horcruxes. Next, his charm. He was able to convince hordes of wizards, creatures, and even humans to join his cause. He offered them positions of powers or manipulation to get him to join his side.

His hatred for mudbloods (wizards that did not come from wizarding families or are half wizard-half human) is what ultimately makes Voldemort a terrifying character. He aims to destroy all the mudbloods because his human father rejected him, and he was bullied by the children at the orphanage.

Finally, his image. How J.K. Rowling describes him is disturbing. Voldemort has red eyes with slitted pupils, has pale white skin, is tall, and dresses in a flowy, black robe. That image alone is enough to send anyone running.

✎ HOW THE PROTAGONIST CAN DEFEAT THE VILLAIN

After you have given your antagonist a motivation and have defined them, now you must decide how your protagonist can defeat them. It's imperative you give your antagonist a flaw or a weakness. Without a flaw, your protagonist will either overcome them with ease or have a difficult time defeating them (unless that is the point of the story).

Here are some examples of antagonists' flaws or weaknesses.

In Warriors, Tigerstar's flaw ambition was also his biggest weakness. He wanted so desperately to become leader that he allied himself with a dangerous clan leader who eventually murdered him. In Bewitching, Lisette's jealousy led to her being publicly rejected by a celebrity who chose Emma over her.

Inanimate force and internal type antagonists can have weaknesses, too. In Tokyo Ghoul, the CCG's weakness is that their knowledge on ghouls is limited. Ghouls blend into human society so well that it's difficult to find a problematic one. In Crank, Kristina's addiction was crippled by her eventual reconnection with her mother and having a baby.

While it's easy coming up with an antagonist, it may be tricky creating an antagonist that truly hinders the protagonist. Once you have learned how to create an antagonist, you may still find it difficult to create the perfect antagonist. However, by defining what makes them an antagonist, giving them a motivation, and giving them a weakness/flaw, you are on your way to creating a memorable antagonist that your audience will love to hate.

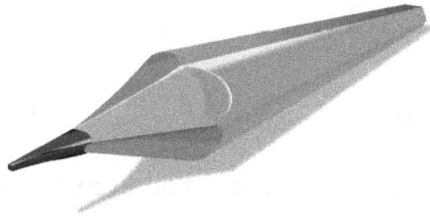

CHAPTER 8

STORYLINE

Ask an adult what their favourite book growing up was, and more times than not, they will list a picture book. Why? Because picture books are the first books we are exposed to, and for some, it's the only books we've ever read. This means as a writer, there is a lot of pressure when you plot your picture book because you need to create a memorable storyline.

But how do you build a plot in only 32 pages? Let me show you!

HOW TO WRITE THE PLOT FOR A PICTURE'S BOOK

From fantasy to mystery to comedy, the same genres that adults read are often appealing to children. However, book plots in children's literature deal with different subject matter than stories written for adults and contain storylines that are less complex and intense. If you're considering becoming a children's book author, it may be helpful to keep the following tips in mind:

Think like a kid.

The topics that may interest you as an adult may not be as compelling to a young reader. Think back to your own experiences as a kid to help inspire book ideas. Your fears, memories, and feelings are all viable fodder for your own children's stories. Your plot should include themes that can be universally understood by most children: loneliness, lack of parental understanding, anxiety over making new friends, or any first-time experiences you also went through while growing up. Relatable themes can help you develop your plot, allowing you to accurately set up the story for your young readers.

Know the market.

Depending on the type of picture book you're writing, certain subgenres might be more appealing to book editors and literary agents. For instance, science fiction or romance might be hot categories for young adult novels, or paranormal adventure might be what's currently popular for middle-grade books. As a children's picture book writer, it's important to know what kind of books your young audience is hungry for—especially because kids' attention spans do not lend them the patience to stick with something that doesn't excite them or immediately grab their interest.

Create a relatable main character.

While creating a relatable main character is a good thing for all novels regardless of the target audience, young children like to read about memorable characters who are closer in age to themselves. They enjoy reading about kids just like them who do heroic things or experience similar growing pains—they would likely not be entertained by or understand the plight and point of view of a 65-year-old. Your storyline should be driven by protagonists who possess simple qualities young children can understand, like courage, kindness, and the ability to make things fun. That doesn't mean the main characters moving your story forward cannot have flaws or undesirable traits, but that they are still redeemable in a way that the readers in your target age range will root for and empathize with despite their shortcomings. Without these elements, your audience is left with a barebones premise—a sequence of events untethered by character development or emotional arcs. This may not be a priority when writing picture books for infants, but many early readers and older children can follow and be entertained by a character's change as a story progresses.

Read more children's books.

Writing picture books requires knowing how to write in a way children understand. While simple themes and unsophisticated sentence structure are both good ways to immerse your young audience, there are other elements to consider when writing books for children—like pacing and development. A good children's book can help you figure out how to approach your own story structure. Read the best books for kids by bestselling authors and see how they integrate their premise into their world. Which chapter does the hero get their call to action? When do the protagonist and villain come face to face for the first time? Use this knowledge to inform your structure when writing the plot to your own book.

CHAPTER 9

JOURNEYS AND QUESTS

F or very young children, even a trip to a grocery store can be thrilling. Cheese samples, the fish department, and the dewy surprise of automatic misting in the produce section: Lots of marvels are packed in those prosaic aisles. Some of the most enduring children's books transform something ordinary — a purple crayon, a wardrobe, a red pebble — into vehicles for exhilarating journeys.

The quest narrative is one of the oldest and surest ways of telling a story and everyone, young or old, loves an adventure story. What better way to draw in the attention of young readers than making use of this concept? This takes skills to successfully incorporate because writing children's quest and adventures requires a vivid imagination, strong writing skills, and the ability to put yourself in the mind of a child. How do you write a gripping fantasy adventure for children?

✎ YOU NEED TO BRAINSTORM FIRST.

There are so many ideas to pick from. You can create a list of ideas no matter how strange they sound, write it down.

Next, decide on whether you want your readers to take an active or laid-back part in the quest. Will you be writing using the first- or third-person pronoun?

What brings about a compelling quest is making sure your story has an inciting incident. What will your quest be all about? Will your protagonist battle monsters, pirates, or aliens? Will it be about travel to medieval times or a dream world? Will your story be about having superpowers? Think of an event that will change or challenge the protagonist. This event can come from or be caused by monsters, aliens, evil spirits, a band of pirates or marauders, secret societies, or even nature.

A great way tool to use is the **pick-a-path** or **choose your own adventure** style of writing.

A Pick-a-Path story is almost always written in the second person ("you") which draws the reader into the story. The pages are numbered, even in manuscript form. The opening story is not extremely detailed, just enough to let the reader get the lay of the land. There is very little fleshing out to do. The story is always exciting, and that excitement is what moves it along, making the reader anxious to get from one chapter to the next.

When writing in the second person, you will always have to check yourself (and relentlessly proofread!) to make sure you are addressing your reader as "you" so that they feel they are inside the story. That is the easy part!

The hard part is writing the same story with multiple endings.

Here's how Pick-A-Path stories work:

The reader reads the first chapter - this is where you address the reader as the main character, create your setting, give a basic plot, add a friend or two for supporting characters and dump your reader into a dilemma.

For the story to continue, the reader is offered a minimum of three choices at the end of each chapter to determine where the story will go next. These are called "jumps." You can make your first chapter about two to three pages long to give the reader enough of a picture so he can climb into the story, or you can decide to make your opening chapter one to two pages, starting the action and decisions immediately.

If you choose to write: Know your subject matter and your story will flow that much easier.

Write a dramatic climax. The climax is the high point of your story. Convey and describe how your protagonist is dealing with the situation he's/she's in, how the event impacts him/her and the people around. Highlight the major decision or choice he/she is going to make, as well as the eventual consequence. Your climax should be full of drama and action.

Write a fantastic ending. Even if the problem or conflict is resolved, your story is not quite finished. So, you might want to wrap it up in an interesting manner. You can end your fantasy adventure by showing the moral (or important lesson) through the actions of your protagonist or making reference to a theme, such as friendship, teamwork, or courage.

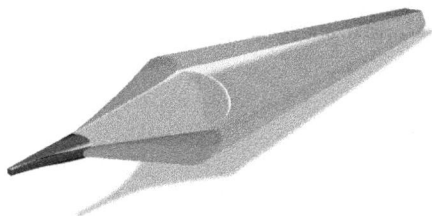

CHAPTER 10

THEMES AND MESSAGES

✎ WHAT DO CHILDREN WANT FROM A STORY?

Children want three basic elements in a story: suspense, characters who are believable, and characters who act to solve problems. We find our themes in the problems.

Superficially speaking, children like stories that include adventure, mystery, excitement, discovery, daring, novelty, and humour. They want to know that there are ways to cope with dilemmas. We must offer ideas and strategies that show children they are not alone.

We will be looking into a list of themes that deal with issues that are important to this youthful audience. They cover the anxieties, fears, and desires that children experience. There are many plots you can choose as vehicles for these stories, but all of them need the protagonist to find a way to address a problem.

✎ WHAT IS A THEME?

A theme can be found by answering one, or both, of these questions:

- ▲ What does the protagonist learn about him or herself in the story?

- ▲ What does the protagonist learn to cope with in the story?

✎ FRIENDSHIP

Friendship is a very common need for children and therefore, any book that uses this theme is desirable reading. An example is "The Outsiders" by S.E. Hinton, which deals with friendship as part of gang life. The story develops the theme with a gang from a low-income area and one from an affluent one. Fights are as much a part of their lives as competition for girls. Changes in the character's lives focus upon the necessity for friendship and the need for being part of a group. Another book on this theme is "Bad Fall" by Charles Crawford. This story shows the importance of friendship between two young boys.

✎ FAMILY

All families are different, and yet there is something common in family life. For example, the book, "Everywhere" by Bruce Brooks show the relationship between a young boy and his aging grandfather. In "The Stone-Faced Boy" by Paula Fox, the young boy seems to be rejected by his family and only as a result of coping with difficult situations does his family come to accept him.

✎ BRAVERY AND COURAGE

Bravery and courage are often the focus of children's books. The Harry Potter book series by J.K. Rowling illustrates the universal appeal of this theme, beyond even the audience of children. Adults and children alike are inspired by the bravery and courage of Harry and his friends throughout their many adventures.

✎ COMPASSION FOR OTHERS

Compassion is a recurrent theme in children's literature. In Uncle Willie and the Soup Kitchen, author DyAnne Disalvo Ryan seeks to encourage children to feel compassion for those who depend on the kindness of others for survival. The author has real-world experience as a soup kitchen volunteer, so the book is based on a unique perspective on volunteering in a soup kitchen, as well as depending on one for sustenance.

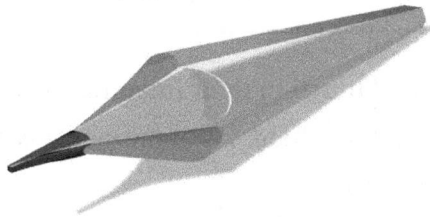

CHAPTER 11

THE SOUND OF THE WORDS

One of the joys of reading picture books aloud is all the funny noises you get to make while telling the story. A great picture book can have you tooting like a locomotive, clacking like typewriters, and crunching like a voracious rabbit.

Besides being a doozy of a spelling word, onomatopoeia — words that represent sounds — is ideally suited for kids' books. Whether it's the "wee-ooh! wee-ooh!" of a fire engine or the "cheep! cheep!" of a little chick, sound words can bring books to life for children. There's an educational benefit, sand imitating sound words helps children build phonological awareness, a key aspect of early literacy development.

✎ PROBLEMS WITH USING SOUNDS

Before we discuss the right ways to use sounds, let's talk about some of the problems with this tool. One of the main issues is the overuse of sounds. We want to include the five senses when we describe scenes. We want our readers to not only see our stories, but to use their sense of smell, taste, sound, and touch in their imaginations to fully experience the world we have built for them. Onomatopoeia is an effective way to include the sense of sound.

The overuse of sounds typically comes from too many interjections or one-word sentences. These can affect the pacing of your writing and jolt your reader out of the story. Repetition can quickly become cliché.

Word choice is another issue with onomatopoeia. The words you use to describe sound should match the tone, target age group, and genre of your book. Often, onomatopoeia interjections are used more commonly in middle-grade and young adult fiction. The diction must be simpler and easier to read for younger readers who don't have an advanced vocabulary.

Onomatopoeia is by no means meant only for young audiences but be mindful that the word you choose matches the tone of your writing. A plop is a great descriptor for comedic writing or contemporary, informal scenes. Plops of water do not, however, fit in a dramatic scene in a Medieval-inspired fantasy world.

✎ EFFECTIVE USE OF ONOMATOPOEIA

So, we know what to avoid doing. But how can we use this tool to make our descriptions more powerful?

Choose sound words to flow in your sentences. Onomatopoetic words can be used as verbs, nouns, and even adjectives. Using these words is far more effective than just sprinkling in interjections. It won't pull your reader out of the story because it's part of the overall flow of your descriptions.

✎ COMMON SOUND WORDS & LETTER COMBINATIONS

Many times, you can tell what an onomatopoeic word is describing based on letter combinations contained within the word. These combinations usually come at the beginning, but a few also come at the end. The following examples have been grouped according to how they are used.

✎ VERBS AS ONOMATOPOEIA

Description isn't just about adjectives. Choosing powerful, active verbs is the best way to show instead of telling. They allow the reader to fully experience a scene and help set the tone. They also add specificity to your writing.

Let's look at some examples of onomatopoetic verbs:

- ◢ He flipped a switch, and the furnace roared to life.

- ◢ The cabinet doors were opened, revealing forgotten plates and chipped mugs. Trash overflowed from the garbage can, and flies buzzed around it. Water dripped from the faucet into the dirty sink.

- ◢ She gasped as she looked out the window. He was home.

- ◢ He hissed at me to get away from him. I took a step back. He was trembling, and he panted in pain. Fear shone from his bruised eyes, and blood dribbled from the corner of his mouth.

✎ NOUNS AS ONOMATOPOEIA

Verbs aren't the only words we can use for sounds. There are plenty of onomatopoetic words that can be used as nouns. Again, these add a degree of realness and specificity to your descriptions.

Here are some examples:

- ◢ A crash sounded from the opposite room, followed by scrapes and clangs.

- ◢ He jumped into the water after me with a splash and a euphoric chortle.

- ◢ In December, the shops are filled with chatter and jingles and friendly greetings of "Happy Holidays."

✎ ADJECTIVES AS ONOMATOPOEIA

Onomatopoetic adjectives should be used sparingly, but can be highly effective:

- ◢ The middle-school teachers avoided the hallway with the cacophonous band and orchestra classes.

- ◢ The barn was full of squealing pigs and bleating sheep.

- ◢ I walked through the drizzling rain and rumbling thunder.

Use them when you want the reader to pay particular attention to the manner of the environment in your story.

Sounds don't have to be complicated or make your readers cringe. When used correctly and effectively, it can be a powerful literary device to enrich your story. As writers, one of our main jobs is to bring the words on the page to life for our readers. Spice up your descriptions with some tone-appropriate onomatopoeia, and make your next work hit the shelves with a bang!

CHAPTER 12

PATTERNED LANGUAGE

Ever been around children? You will notice they love to find and create patterns? They're not alone. Many kids love to search for patterns in the world around them. Pattern recognition is a key step in developmental learning, and it also teaches kids basic math concepts.

In case you need a refresher, patterns are things that repeat in a logical way. You can find them in music, art, nature, math, and even sports. From clapping to colouring, patterns are everywhere!

Even our youngest children can recognize patterns and use categories to process new information. Almost everything we see, hear, or touch contains details that our brain processes. Without realizing it, our brain is looking for what is new, what is different, and what has changed. New information is matched to a category that already exists in our mind.

Patterns can be comforting to young readers. They help them understand what comes next, bringing a bit of order to their chaotic world. Nursery rhymes and lullabies are full of repetition and rhymes are a great example of how children develop memory recall and make predictions.

In the book, Pitter Pattern by Joyce Hesselberth, expertly makes use of basic patterns in nature, music, sports, art, language, and math. When three children come inside after a rainstorm, they observe their tasty-looking snack and say:

Milk, apple, cracker, cheese.

Milk, apple, cracker, cheese.

Milk, apple, cracker cheese.

There are patterns everywhere!

How many can you find?

This need to find order, to compare and contrast, and to pay attention to what remains the same is an important part of early learning, one that can be taken advantage of to write a compelling picture book. Young readers will learn to find patterns in letters and words and would often use this information to read groups of words (for example, sun, fun, bun all contain the '-un' letter pattern or family).

As the plot builds, readers will be able to accurately predict and read (even fake read) the repetitive text because they'll know it's coming. Even for younger children who are non-readers, patterns give an important predictability.

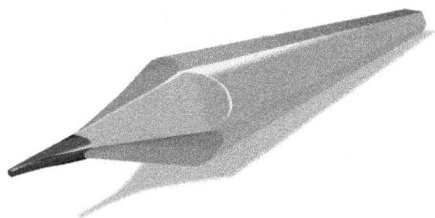

CHAPTER 13

RHYME

If you're wondering how to write a rhyming picture book, you're not alone. Many writers are drawn to this format. Rhyming is, after all, a nostalgic and famed feature of picture books. Maybe you grew up with nursery rhymes, or maybe rhyming simply feels ideal. When done well, rhyming picture books are snappy, quotable, and fun to read. Children retain the words more easily and begin to identify patterns and sounds: a real treat. The problem? Writing a good rhyming picture book is much trickier than it looks.

I've always loved writing rhymes, even as a little girl. It's not only fun, but you can also get a huge amount of satisfaction from finding the perfect rhyme to tell a joke or move the story along. It's not always easy though. Sometimes it can take a lot of thinking to get a line just right.

Writing a good rhyming story is a bit like doing a jigsaw. When I begin, I know what the whole story will be (so that's like the finished picture) and I must put the pieces (or the words) together in exactly the right way to make everything fit. Just as it would be with a jigsaw, you can't shove a piece into a place it doesn't fit because otherwise, in the end, the picture will be wonky.

For some people, writing brilliant rhyme comes naturally – but for other people, practice makes perfect. Here are my top tips for writing a rollicking rhyming story.

✎ THE STORY SHOULD COME FIRST

When you're writing in rhyme, it's easy to become obsessed with finding the ending words that go together. But if you concentrate on the rhyme more than you do on the plot, you'll probably end up with a story that doesn't feel all that satisfying. It might not have a good focus, or make sense, or be as entertaining as it should be. The rule to remember is the story is just as important as the rhyme.

Here's a slightly silly example (which I just made up!) showing how you can easily sacrifice the focus of a story for rhyme:

Here's a dungeon, oh so scary.

Don't go down there! Please be wary!

You must NOT wander in the dark,

Especially not if you're a shark!

The first three lines set up a story, which has focus. Oooh! It's all about a scary dungeon! Too scary to enter! But then… hey, what the lollypop is a shark doing in this rhyme? A shark especially shouldn't go in a dungeon. Huh? It makes no sense! The only reason the shark shows up in this rhyme is because it goes with 'dark'. But it makes you think, 'errrr…' and by that point, you've forgotten all about the scary dungeon! The shark has sacrificed the story for the rhyme. Let's get rid of it.

You must NOT wander in the gloom

Of that spooky, dingy room!

I used gloom instead of dark. It means the same thing as dark really – AND I could find a rhyme that made sense in the context of the story.

So, before you even think about the rhyming aspect, write down your story in prose, so you know what is going to happen at the beginning, the middle, and the end (a prose version about a scary dungeon would be VERY unlikely to have a shark in it!). Once you have that, you can start doing your 'jigsaw', finding the perfect words. And when you've finished, your rhyming story will have focus and make sense.

✏ PERFECT OR IMPERFECT?

There are lots of definitions to describe different types of rhyme – for example, people talk about half rhyme, slant rhyme, near rhyme, assonance, and consonance. But to keep things simple, let's just talk about perfect and imperfect rhyme – and which of the two you want to use.

Perfect rhyme is harder by nature because it requires the rhyming words to match in both their vowel and consonant sounds. So, the combination of eat/sweet matches both the "ee" sound and the "t" sound. Similarly host/most share both the "oh" sound and the "st" sound.

If you were using imperfect rhyme, though, you might choose to only match either the vowel sound, OR the consonant sound. So, you could have eat/leaf, which share only the "ee" sound. Or you could have host/last which share only the "st" sound.

Put simply, there are more imperfect rhyme combinations in the English language than there are perfect rhyme combinations – so writing in imperfect rhyme will give you more options. Writing in perfect rhyme is harder and takes more practice, so don't feel bad about starting out with imperfect rhyme, pop stars use it all the time! Think about some of the lyrics to some of your favourite songs, and I bet you find loads of examples of imperfect rhyme.

✎ MASTER RHYTHM

Did you know that poems have feet? No? Well, if you were to learn about poetry in a formal way, you'd be bombarded by all sort of funny terms which are used to describe the way verse is written, including metric feet, meter, and iambs. It can all get very technical, but you don't necessarily need to know that stuff. All you need to understand is that poems and rhymes normally have rhythm.

If you listen to a rhyming poem being read aloud, you'll probably be able to detect the rhythm, or a beat, running through it It's a bit like listening to a tune being played.

But if, when writing rhyme, you somehow miss a beat of your rhythm, it feels awkward. Imagine listening to your favourite pop star singing your favourite song – but they have hiccups. Argh! That's what it feels like when a rhyme loses its beat.

Being consistent with your rhythm can be tricky and it has a lot to with the emphasis we put on syllables in words and phrases – it is these strong and weak syllables which provide the rhythm. When we speak naturally, we put more emphasis on some syllables than we do on others. See how I have made the stronger syllables bold?

When you write a line of rhyme, it's important not to force the reader to put the emphasis on a syllable where it wouldn't occur in natural speech, just to achieve the rhythm. For example, if you put stress on the last part of the word emphasis, it would sound weird and awkward. So, you need to try to write the lines of your rhyming story so all the words can be read in a natural, but rhythmic way.

✎ TEST YOUR RHYMING STORY

Have you written a brilliant rhyming story? I find a very good way to find out is to ask someone to read your work aloud to you. Listen carefully. Do they stumble on any lines? Do they pause in parts? These clues will let you know if you have some bits and pieces that need fixing.

Perhaps you need to add a syllable to fix your rhythm, or maybe you need to take one away. It might be that you need to swap one word for another, to make sure the syllable emphasis falls in the right place for your rhyme's beat.

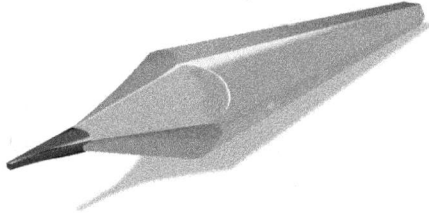

CHAPTER 14

DIALOGUE

Dialogue is a powerful device for storytelling. Some of the best dialogue out there moves a story along and develops three-dimensional and complex characters. Don't underestimate dialogue; it's so much more than a couple of characters talking to each other.

How to write dialogue? That's something that should come naturally. After all, most of us spend at least a portion of each day in conversation with other people. But creating dialogue is more than simply transcribing actual speech. It's even more complicated in children's books, because the age of the reader must also be taken into consideration.

Written dialogue is a compressed form of real speech; it's the meat of the conversation with all the fillers removed. Picture books and easy readers–books written for children ages eight and under–are told primarily through action, and the dialogue reflects this action. The characters' speech in these books must give a sense of their personalities, but also clue the reader into what's happening in the story. Just as plot has a forward direction, so must the dialogue.

In Arthur's Loose Tooth, an easy reader by Lillian Hoban, Arthur's dilemma is presented to the reader through a portion of a conversation with his sister:

"Guess what we are having for dessert," said Violet.

"It is your favourite treat! It is taffy apples!"

"Taffy apples!" said Arthur.

"I can't eat taffy apples with a loose tooth!

It might get stuck in the taffy!"

"Well, if it gets stuck, you can pull it out," said Violet.

"I don't want to pull it out," said Arthur.

Using simple, complete sentences necessary in an easy reader, the author has revealed the story's action through natural-sounding dialogue. But how to write dialogue as stories get longer and more complicated? In these cases, the back-and-forth chatter between characters can be less linear. In real life, each person brings his or her own viewpoint into the conversation and gets something different out of the exchange. Allowing the dialogue to bounce around naturally can add humour to the scene and go a long way toward character development. However, you still need to be mindful of giving the reader new information that supports the plot.

How then can you write a compelling dialogue?

✎ LISTEN A LOT

One of the hardest things about writing children's dialogue can be trying to make it sound natural. You know what you want your characters to say or think, but often it comes off as awkward or unnatural.

The only way to get a feel for natural dialogue is to listen to how other people (kids included), speak and communicate with each other. For this, it's perfectly okay to eavesdrop!

If you are not a parent, guardian, teacher, aunt, or uncle, or don't work with kids in any capacity, go somewhere where you'll be able to hear an abundance of conversation with children, like a mall, park, or restaurant. Then, pay close attention to speech and how they talk.

No two people speak the same, let alone children. Some speak fast, others slow. Older children, such as middle schoolers and preteens, may have an extensive vocabulary while others, such as kids in primary school, use simpler words. Also, take note of any accents or unique ways people around you talk.

✎ GET IN THE MIND OF YOUR CHARACTERS

Just like how no two children are the same, your characters shouldn't be, either. Hopefully, you've given them distinct, unique personalities and mannerisms. These points should transfer into their speech.

There are several things that come with this. Consider where they're from. Do they have any accents or slang they like to use? Do they have a favourite word they use frequently? Maybe they don't talk much or, depending on their age, they don't have a large vocabulary.

These are all aspects you should be thinking about that will determine how you write your dialogue effectively.

✎ LEAVE OUT THE UNIMPORTANT STUFF

Dialogue is just as important as any other storytelling element. It should always be used to either move your children's story along or develop your children's book characters. Everything your characters talk about or say to each other should fulfil a goal or reveal something about the character. In other words, leave out the filler if it doesn't have a purpose.

Two characters rambling about cakes with no clear reason as to why they're talking about it is dull. But maybe "Thirteen-year-old-twins Margo and Vivian" are arguing which flavour to ask their parents to get for their upcoming birthday party. A little more intriguing, right?

And what if they aren't even upset about the cake, but something else, something they're not saying but only hinting at. What if one of them doesn't even wish to have the birthday party and is delicately trying to point this out. That's much more compelling, isn't it?

Now, we have a story going and dialogue to drive the plot along. Through what's said (and often, what isn't) we have a clear direction of where we're going.

Dialogue is a fascinating story element that adds another layer of intricacy to your story–if you know how to use it effectively.

These points would help you to write stunning dialogue for your children's books should help you craft realistic and purposeful conversations.

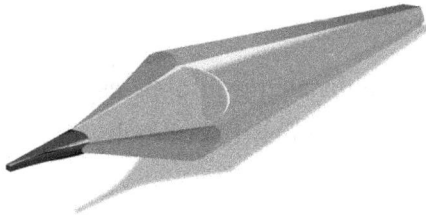

CHAPTER 15

HUMOUR

Funny books are memorable. They are a joy to share with young readers, and often have a laugh for grown-ups too! That is why everywhere I look on editor and agent submission wish list these days, I read the following: WANTED: Funny, Quirky Picture Books. Why? Because everyone enjoys a laugh—kids and adults alike. Laughing makes people feel good, and as a result, funny sells.

But if you're not the kind of person who automatically sees the funny side of life, you may find writing humorous picture books difficult. (And even if you do see the funny side of life, like me, you may still find it a struggle.)

JUXTAPOSITION

Put two things together that don't normally go together. This already sets the scene for a humorous story before you've even written a word. For example, Melinda Long puts 'pirates' and 'a baby' together in Pirates Don't Change Diapers (illustrated by David Shannon). Who can resist laughing at babysitting pirates, especially when they think they've been given the task of sitting on babies?

✎ CONTRADICTIONS

Some of the funniest books to read are those in which the illustrations contradict the text. Mark Teague does this so well in his book, Dear Mrs. LaRue: Letters from Obedience School. In the book, Ike begs to be rescued from dog obedience school. He writes letters home to Mrs. LaRue, complaining about the school and painting a bleak picture of it, while the colour illustrations tell a very different picture—that of a luxury, high-class school that is more akin to a spa retreat.

✎ GIVE IT A TWIST

Another way to ensure your book is humorous is to add a twist. Your book should be anything but predictable, so surprise your audience. A recent book I've read that accomplishes this is I Thought This was a Bear Book by Tara Lazar and Benji Davies. The entire book is a twisted fairy tale with an alien accidentally falling into the pages of Goldilocks and the Three Bears. But while some of the elements in the book, like the appearance of Goldilocks, porridge, chairs, and beds are expected, these elements are mish-mashed with the story of the alien, making for a completely new and unpredictable book. And just when you think you've got the book sussed and the happy ending is looming, a further twist shows up on the last page. But to find out what it is, you'll have to read the book!

✎ ILLUSTRATIONS

Illustrations are another way to inject humour into your picture book. However, since this is a post about writing, rather than illustrating, I'm not going to say much here, except occasionally–and only very occasionally–if you come up with a strong, visual image that would enhance the humour in your text, then you might want to consider inserting an illustration note in your manuscript.

Humour is subjective so employing these tricks is no guarantee that everyone will find your book humorous, but you're sure to tickle a few funny bones.

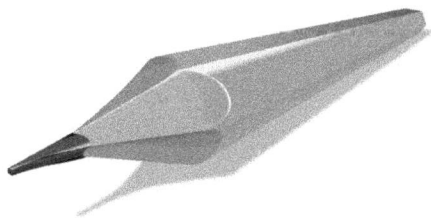

CHAPTER 16

ENDINGS

Wouldn't it be great if there were a magic 'ending machine'? You'd write your picture book and then feed it in and POOF! – out pops a spectacular ending!

Endings can be one of the most frustrating and niggle some aspects of writing picture books. But when you've cracked it, a great ending can make the difference between that book that children ask for again and again, and the one they aren't really fussed about ever reading again.

So, what makes a great ending?

✎ HAVE A PLAN FOR YOUR ENDING

This is a big one. We will already want to have an ending in mind during the entire writing process. Simply hoping to just come up with a perfect ending won't work. Or at least not as well as if it were planned.

The way you're planning to end your story may change or evolve over time, and that's perfectly okay. But always try to keep an end in mind as you're writing your story. It will give you something to work toward. A beacon that will help you let your story end on a high and touching note.

Sometimes, it takes me days, weeks even, to come up with just the right ending. The key is not to rush it. Unless it feels just right, it isn't the perfect ending.

Never settle! You will want that punch, that feeling that your ending does your story justice. I usually know and feel it when I've found the right ending, and the right wording.

If it moves you when you write it, it will most definitely move and touch your readers.

✎ THE RIGHT WORDING MATTERS

Remember that we're talking about picture books here. We generally only have about 1 to 2 sentences to 'deliver' our perfect ending. And that means that every word counts. So again, don't rush it.

When asking yourself how to end a story, be sure to dedicate some time to this. I like taking my general idea, jot it down onto a piece of paper or on a new page on my computer, and then come up with different ways of saying the exact same thing. Sometimes, all it takes is the shifting or reordering of words or replacing one word with another will do the trick.

It isn't uncommon that I end up with about 50 different versions of my ending. So don't get discouraged if you haven't found your ending after only a couple of tries. Your little readers want to be moved. Their parents or other caregivers that are reading the book to their little ones want to be moved. So go for the heart. Don't settle.

✎ A REAL ENDING OF THE STORY

Your story ending for your children's book should have a real ending. Don't leave your little readers hanging. Kids like solutions and resolutions.

Did Teddy make it?
Did Panda get his cookie?
Did the boy find his dad?

Little kids don't yet know how to handle cliff-hangers or how to draw their own conclusions. There should be no teaser, but rather a definite and satisfying ending.

This doesn't mean that your story needs to have a happy ending. We just want to make sure that our little readers know exactly what happened, and that all questions have been answered and resolved.

✎ CENTER STAGE AND SPOTLIGHTS

No matter how long or short our picture book story ends up being, for our ending, we will want to make sure that our main character takes centre stage. It's the main character the little readers have come to know and love, so it should be this character that brings the story to a close. That's what will ultimately help you make your story feel complete to the reader.

✎ YOUR MESSAGE & PURPOSE

Weaving our book's message or purpose into the ending will make our story feel complete, like it has come full circle. Not only will it satisfy our little readers, but also the grownups that are reading this book with or to their children.

If you've got a story with a dramatic and emotional arc and you've chosen the right plot and characters, the end of that winning combination should be one of the easiest things to write. If you're struggling, maybe go back to the middle and see if the problem isn't hiding there.

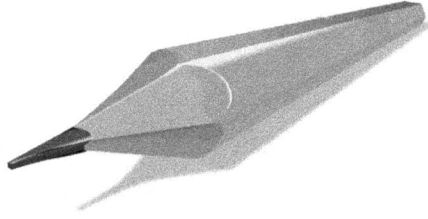

CHAPTER 17

NUMBERS, LETTERS, COLOURS

It is a known fact that picture books are capable of introducing toddlers and young children to the world, through colours, shapes, numbers, letters and more.

It's never too early to read to children and parent usually make use of picture books are a great introduction to first concepts, perfect for even the youngest babies.

Through colour, touch, sound, and shapes young children start to make sense of the world around them and these picture books turn out to be old gems that every nursery bookshelf should have.

Books that introduce children to numbers, letters and colours are called concept books. Concept books are a type of picture book that introduces basic ideas, or concepts, to young children. They are sometimes described as informational picture books for pre-schoolers. These books present single, concrete concepts such as alphabet, colours, numbers and counting, shapes and opposites.

Concept books play an important part in early literacy and can be found in almost all children's collections and if you want your picture book to be a hit amongst parents and teachers, making use of number, letters and colours is a great idea.

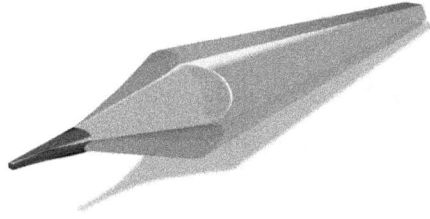

CHAPTER 18

INCLUSIVITY: REFLECTING THE WORLD

Inclusion in books matters because literature conveys sociocultural norms that can shape children's beliefs and aspirations, and influence how they see and understand themselves and their place in the world. Besides, having children's lived experiences portrayed in the books they read is good for learning overall. An emotional connection to a book can motivate readers, especially reluctant ones.

Quiet! by Kate Alizadeh is a powerful example of how a picture book can create an effortlessly inclusive backdrop and reflect our diverse community whilst avoiding either a forced or tokenistic approach.

Here are a few ideas on adding characters naturally and positively with an inclusive lens and avoiding some of the potential pitfalls.

THINK BEYOND WHEELCHAIRS

The international symbol for disability is a wheelchair, so it's hardly surprising it is the first thing that comes to mind when we picture disabled characters. In fact, less than 8% of disabled people in the UK are wheelchair users.

There are so many forms of disability which are under-represented – in fact, some have seldom (if ever) appeared in a children's book. Isn't it time that they did?

✎ AVOID TOKENISM

The inclusion of characters from marginalized communities should involve them having meaningful roles in the story. It is not inclusive to have these characters as inactive observers. In an analysis of more than 1,100 award-winning children's books in the US, female characters were "seen more than heard", indicating a symbolic inclusion in pictures without a substantive inclusion in the story.

In the South African story, The Suitcase, by Mbongeni Nzimande, illustrated by Elizabeth Pulles, the protagonist, Lwazi, needs something to wear to participate in a dance competition. Not only is Lwazi an albino child, but the reader would not know this without the illustrations.

The story focuses on something universally relatable: wanting something that one does not have. This emphasis on the humanity we all share, regardless of our differences, builds empathy for marginalized communities.

✎ FACE AND SKIN

How often have you seen someone with facial disfiguration, cleft palate, eczema, or a birthmark in a children's book? This is still a particularly under-represented area in books, but particularly in those for younger readers. Including a child with a birthmark or skin disorder doesn't have to be presented as an "issue" but just something that appears naturally, as it might well do in any classroom or nursery. And it's not as difficult as you might think – there's plenty of reference material out there to help.

✎ COMPLEX NEEDS

Characters with profound and multiple difficulties have rarely appeared in children's books, and, where they have, it is generally in an issue book or a book "about" disability.

Surely such children can also be included equally and without comment alongside their peers, with just a bit of research and thought?

✎ CHALLENGE STEREOTYPES IN CULTURALLY SENSITIVE WAY

Children's books can challenge stereotypes, such as having female characters in roles that are usually associated with men. While it is important to raise questions and encourage critical reflection about the status quo, local book creators should decide how and in what way they want to push boundaries for their own creative works.

The danger to imposing diversity requirements on book creators is that the resulting stories risk being only symbolically inclusive, and they might not be sensitive to the local context.

Finally, it is not enough for a picture book to have inclusive representation within it, but every child needs to be able to access it. Ensuring book access for all will require book adaptations such as the development of braille books, audio books, and minority language translations.

With nobody left out, we may realize a dream in which inclusive books, that are as diverse as the human experience, are available to all children to read with ease, understanding and enjoyment.

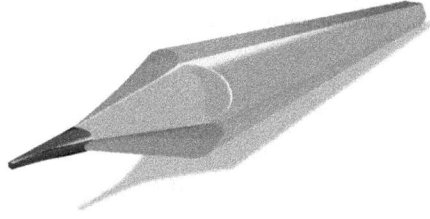

CHAPTER 19

THE ROLE OF THE ILLUSTRATOR

A children's book illustrator creates imagery for children's books, working closely with the author to bring stories to life with original illustrations that appeal to the book's age demographic. In children's books, images can provide context clues and help children understand what they're reading.

The main purpose of illustration is to get a message across to the readers or viewers. Some of the illustrations are absolutely breath taking but their job is to elaborate and clarify the meaning of the text. In the books meant for children, illustrations are used to make the children learn how to read. Illustrations can transform a simple story into an exciting and fascinating one.

Sometimes, illustrations are a critical component of a book. Illustrations can show how an important scene in the book looks. History tomes can give the reader a peek into the past by showing pictures and maps from a particular time or area. In children's books, illustrations can help a child learn to establish verbal and visual connections. In business books, illustrations such as charts, graphs, and diagrams, can help convey complex concepts.

Can an illustrator play a role in developing a book? Yes, of course he can! Even if he is directed to transform certain scenes into pictures, the illustrator is the one who will interpret those scenes and draw them in his own style. An artist might also choose additional scenes to illustrate (if he is given the latitude to do so). Another way an illustrator is involved in book development is in the timing of the project. A publisher can't finalize, print, or bind a book without having the illustrations in hand. If illustrations come in late, then the book's printing and release are likely to be delayed.

Does an illustrator impact the content? The answer is not clear cut. Two factors govern the extent of an illustrator's impact. First, what is the book about? If it's a picture book with little text, then the illustrator is likely to have some real input. The second factor is how early in the writing process the illustrator comes on board. If he begins working with the author early on, then he might be able to influence the actual writing. If he comes in at the end of the writing process, then the illustrator is unlikely to have any input into the creation of the book.

Another issue to consider is who owns the copyright to the illustrations? If you are publishing with the traditional route, the author doesn't buy the copyright. The publisher usually gets rights to the illustrations in the book. According to Dino Art's essay on contracts for illustrators, however, an artist should seek to limit the publisher's copyright license as much as possible. In all contract negotiations each party typically tries to keep as many rights as possible. Copyright ownership is negotiable. So, an artist can continue owning his work if he is a successful negotiator. As an author, if you are self-publishing, the ownership of rights is even further negotiable. You and the illustrator will have to work out the details. Generally, it's good practice for the author to purchase the illustrations and own them outright, as a 'work for hire' product. Consider your intended use of the image and negotiate rights accordingly. For instance, you may be writing a book now, but decide later to add an app related to the book or create a workbook to accompany it. Perhaps you want to use the images in your marketing material for these products. Each of these uses for an illustration is a right that can be negotiated. As with any contract negotiations, I'll recommend you seek advice of legal counsel.

Illustrators can play an important part in the creative process of fashioning a picture book. A writer doesn't always consider the illustrator's role when he is in the midst of writing. When the illustrator appears on the scene, a writer may feel confused and daunted, if he is unfamiliar with the illustrator's role. But now, you should have a grasp of the basic framework in which illustrators operate.

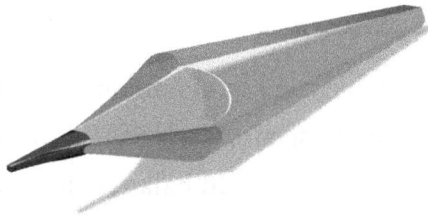

CHAPTER 20

AUTHOR-ILLUSTRATOR TEAMS AND HOW THEY WORK TOGETHER

Illustrators are usually matched with authors by a publishing company. Sometimes, an author will choose an illustrator to work with, especially if they've worked the person before, but whether the author has published once or many times, it is usually the publisher who will pick an illustrator for a book.

The two most common wrong assumptions people make about bookmaking:

Writers and illustrators work together—they don't! Writers write manuscripts and sell these to the publisher. Illustrators promote their illustration work to publishers, who hire them on a contract basis to illustrate the manuscripts they acquire. As always in publishing, there are exceptions to these rules (sometimes you see friends, spouses, siblings' team up), but this is most traditionally how it works. There are a lot of reasons for this which I won't go into here, but mainly the publisher wants to choose text and art to pair together that they believe will have the most successful outcome in finished form. Very well-known authors or illustrators are paid more (in the form of a book advance) for the project, so to balance their budget they might pair that well-known author with a newer illustrator (or vice versa). If you really want to try to work with a partner on your book idea, my advice would be for the you to write the manuscript, the illustrator create a book dummy for it and submit that book dummy as a team to a publisher. Be prepared for the publisher to like the book idea but want to hire their own chosen illustrator for the book. It's your choice to say yes or no to this arrangement.

Writers and illustrators sell their book idea to a publisher by making it first—I remember thinking that to sell a book idea, I had to create a polished, finished version first. Not true! In fact, doing this could really hurt the saleability of the idea. Editors who work at publishing companies are the ones who acquire stories, and they have a lot of great feedback and opinions that will make your idea better. They will ask for revisions—sometimes huge ones! This is a normal part of the bookmaking process. Writers should submit their stories in the form of a Word Doc (no need to format and paginate it like a finished book), and illustrators who have their own story idea to pitch should create a book dummy. This is essentially a loosely pencil-sketched version of the book in PDF form. This gets your idea across and shows your skill with pacing, layouts, page turns, etc. A book dummy should be accompanied with 1-3 pieces of sample finished art, so the art director can get a sense of what the final book would look like.

✎ WHO'S WHO?

The main people an illustrator will be working with at the publishing company are Editors and Art Directors. Writers work with the editor on the story and text, and illustrators work with art directors. If an illustrator is working on their own story, they'll work with both the editor and art director as a team. Some art directors also have a separate designer working on the book who's in charge of the book layout. Of course, there are many other people working in various roles at the publisher, but these are the first two to understand.

✎ HOW DOES A BOOK PROJECT WORK?

After an illustrator is hired to make art for a book (more on that below), the illustrator creates sketches for the book to turn in and discuss with the art director and/or editor. They'll give revision notes, and you'll go back to the drawing board to make a new draft. This might happen a few times, sometimes for the whole book, other times it's certain pages that need more revising than others. Once they get approval on sketches, they'll create the final artwork for the book. Illustrators will do this in their chosen medium, be that painting, drawing, or digital art. If you're working traditionally (painting on paper), most commonly they'll mail the art to the publisher for scanning.

More often, once the art is done, some of the text may become redundant. It's not easy letting favourite phrases go, all those lovely words that I've played with, replaced, and rehearsed…. but if they don't add to the story, they need to go. Let the pictures do their work.

✎ WHICH ILLUSTRATOR?

As already known, combining narrative and imagery unlike any other medium, picture books have the potential to captivate and inspire readers both young and old. Finding an illustrator to bring your vision to life, however, can be a different story entirely.

In the last chapter, we discussed how usually publishers connects the authors with illustrators, you might decide to follow the self-publishing path. With so many options at your fingertips, the question is not where to find illustrators, but how to choose. It's important to know what you're looking for. This may seem backward—you're not an artist, how can you know what kind of art will work for your book? But knowing what you like will focus your search and ensure you get the results you want.

Paint, pencil, pen—each medium has a different look and feel. Browse your local library to see if you're drawn to any specific medium. Then consider the different artists' styles, which Bradley defines as that "difficult-to-define thing that makes the work of one illustrator different from others." It's what makes a fairy tale feel different than an ABC book. The key will be to find an artist working in a medium and style that feels right for your story.

✎ HOW MUCH DOES IT COST?

The short answer is it depends! There's no hard and fast rule. Illustrators' rates are based on their experience and training as well as the amount of time and materials involved. To properly estimate your project, you'll need to know how many illustrations you need which will depend on the number of pages in your project.

You may be thinking, okay, that's all well and good, but how much does it cost? Bestselling author Joanna Penn estimates that the average pay for a 32-page picture book is $3,000 – $12,000, meaning a 32-page book with 20 illustrations equates anywhere from $150 to $600 per illustration. Publishing expert Anthony Puttee estimates a slightly lower standard rate of about $120 per illustration. It really depends on your illustrator's hourly rate and the number of hours it takes for them to complete an illustration, which will depend on the complexity of what you're asking for. It's also worth noting that an illustrator who is willing to work at an extremely low rate is not likely to provide the quality and professionalism you want for your project.

✎ NUTS AND BOLTS: GETTING THE CONTRACT RIGHT

A contract is the best way to make sure that the agreement between author and illustrator is clear. The contract lays out exactly what you're getting for your money, how you'll be working together, and what will happen if anything goes south.

The core of your contract is the project schedule. This should include the exact date for each deliverable, the payment schedule, and a plan for what will happen if a deliverable or payment is late. Don't forget to specify feedback periods and the exact number of revision rounds expected.

Your contract will also cover legal details like crediting, copyright, and royalties. In self-publishing, the author usually pays a flat fee for the illustrator's services, rather than ongoing royalties. When the project is complete and payment has been made in full, the contract specifies that the copyright for the images is transferred to the author to publish, market, and sell their book. The artist may retain some rights to use the images in their portfolio or website. There's usually also a clause stating that if illustrations are reused for other products, such as merchandise, the illustrator gets a certain percentage of the profits as royalties. The contract will also usually include crediting, such as requiring that the illustrator's name appear on the book cover.

✎ DESIGN CONSIDERATIONS

Consider the final design of your book from the start. It'll help you calculate your overall budget, and it will help ensure that your contract with your illustrator is clear and complete.

Be sure you know how you want the text to integrate with the illustrations. If your text will simply sit under each image, you'll probably be able to lay the book out yourself. If you'd like your text integrated within your illustration communicate with your illustrator what you're envisioning.

Likewise know if your illustrator is going to digitize their artwork or mail you physical copies that you'll digitize yourself. When you submit your files, you'll want to make sure the colour is optimized from print.

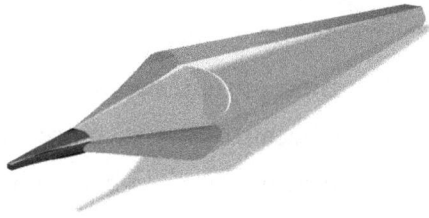

CHAPTER 21

THE AGENT

Writing a book is fun, but getting it published, is where the magic happens. Now, parents can buy your book and children get to read it! It's what all of us authors dream of, right? But how do we exactly publish a children's book? Finding an agent is the next step.

A literary agent works as a mediator between you and the publisher. They will help you get the best contract and negotiate for other things, like foreign rights and media rights. For all this work, they will earn a commission off your writing advance and sales.

To make sure you get a good agent that will find you the best deal, you will need to do your research. Having a bad agent is most of the time worse than not having an agent at all.

WHEN DO YOU NEED AN AGENT?

You will need an agent if you want to submit to a closed house, however, there are other avenues for submission you can try before you submit to one of them.

An offer for either publication or representation is a great way to find an agent you really want because they're more likely to read your query! It will also keep you from signing a bad contract.

✎ WHAT DO YOU SEND TO AN AGENT?

I haven't needed to write a cover letter since most submissions have gone digital, however, you will always need to write a query letter. It's the way to pitch your book to an agent.

Along with the query, most agents will require the first few pages of a novel or full picture book manuscript, plot synopsis, etc. You will need to check their submission requirements before you send to them. It's a rookie move to send the wrong items.

We will discuss the query in detail in the course note.

✎ THE NUMBER ONE TIP TO FIND AN AGENT IS TO DO YOUR RESEARCH!

Agents like queries that are personalized to them, not canned versions. It lets them feel a connection to your story. And it helps you, too!

You don't want to spend time sending to someone that isn't a good fit for you, so take time to do your research before you submit. It's also a way to avoid unnecessary rejection.

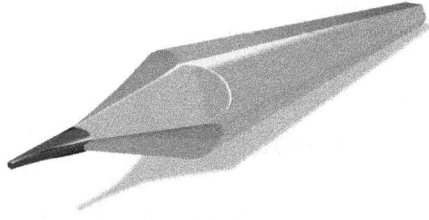

CHAPTER 22

THE EDITOR

You may have heard that you need a book editor or editing services, but what does a book editor do? Book editors can often be mysterious. They work in the shadows, less flashy than literary agents, less public than manuscript creators themselves. We will be breaking down the functions of a book editor so that you can understand a bit more about the masterminds behind the manuscript critique.

What does a book editor do when they work for a publisher? Publishing house editors often operate in relative anonymity unless you really start getting to know the publishing business inside and out. The reason is simple. Most publishing house editors consider projects sent directly by literary agents. They have little incentive to go out there and source material on their own (gone are those good ol' days, alas). So, they appear at writing conferences, give interviews, and make appearances on social media. But for the most part, they're going to work at their respective houses, considering agented submissions, building their house's lists, and growing their relationships with their authors and illustrators. The average writer will not spend a lot of time interacting with "closed house" editors unless they go out on submission with a literary agent or get a book deal.

Editors at publishers that accept unsolicited submissions are a bit different. They want to attract talent, so they may be more public about their wants and personalities, online and at conferences. You may be able to submit to them, so you may interact with them one day, even if you don't have a literary agent.

It's important to remember that, while every editor at a publishing house has their own taste and talent, they work for their publishing house. They must keep their house's particular brand in mind, as well as that of their imprint, and they have to choose projects that they believe will make both artistic and business sense. That's why it can often be a big hurdle to be acquired by a publishing house and to work with one.

✎ WHAT DO EDITORS DO FOR YOU?

More and more, writers are hiring a freelance book editor as part of their goal to publish their work or self-publish. They realize that the publishing landscape is very competitive, and they want to position themselves to make their dreams a reality. Professional feedback—backed by years of experience—is one of the benefits of using a freelance editor. Of course, you must vet the editor very carefully and make sure they're a good fit for you. You also should have some sort of agreement for the service that outlines the scope of work. What do editors do? Well, that depends on what type of editor they are, and what editing services they offer.

Good editors for picture books are familiar with the way young people speak and learn. They can critique and examine illustrations with the fresh eye of a young reader. They also understand the specific trends and nuances of writing for children.

To ensure that your work will appeal to your target audience, they can help you modify your manuscript to suit the reading abilities of children within your target age group. To ensure that your work will appeal to your target audience, they can help you modify your manuscript to suit the reading abilities of children within your target age group.

Editors skilled in this unique genre also understand the basic elements of good fiction—character, conflict, plot, theme, setting and dialogue. In this lesson, we will get into how to get the right book editor for your book.

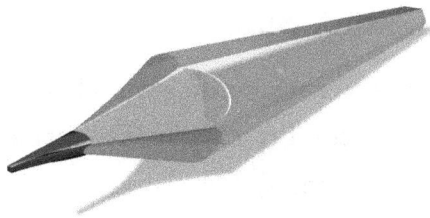

CHAPTER 23

PERFORMANCE AND PROMOTION

Many authors just want to write, and don't want to market. In fact, most despise this aspect of being an author. And this holds true for writers of picture books as well. It is, nonetheless, one of the key factors to your book's success. Without promoting it, it will get lost in the sea of books. A book without the right promotion is like a rocket without fuel.

There are three things that make marketing children's books so different from other genres:

First, children's books are the only type of book where you aren't marketing to your ideal reader.

Since children don't buy books, you must market to adults. That means that your book promotion campaigns must be created with the adult in mind, not the child.

Second, although you are promoting to adults, your book must still appeal to the actual children you wrote the book for.

That means your job as an author is to write a book that appeals to two different audiences: the child (your ideal reader) and the adult book purchaser (your ideal customer).

Finally, the picture book industry distribution channels that are unique to publishing, such as schools and children's libraries.

Despite the differences, marketing a children's book doesn't have to be hard.

Here are some tips to get you started:

1. BEGIN LOCALLY.

The best plan is to begin close to home if you plan to promote a children's book independently. Contact booksellers in your neighbourhood, both chain, and independent stores, to ask if they have a Local Author section and, if yes, request to be included. Offer autographed copies of your book to help spark sales. Stores often put stickers on the covers of signed books to make them more attractive to buyers.

2. HOLD LOCAL EVENTS.

If your book has a theme, offer to host a promotional event (which is different than a passive signing). For example, if your book has a bee character, host an educational presentation on the importance of bees followed by a honey tasting or other hands-on children's activity. Be creative. Interactive events draw kids, parents, and grandparents, and perhaps even the media to the event. Of course, try to sell books while you're there.

3. VISIT LOCAL LIBRARIES.

Many authors are surprised by the role libraries can play in picture book marketing and publicity. Donate copies of your book to your local libraries. Offer to hold a reading at your library. Most libraries provide activities for children. Hosting an interactive event will work here, as well. If the library does not let you sell books on-site (most will not), be sure to hand out bookmarks or business cards directing people to stores or online sellers where your book is available.

4. WORK WITH SCHOOLS AND PRE-SCHOOLS.

Schools are always looking for guest speakers and authors. In most cases, you can arrange to donate books to the school while parents receive order forms for autographed books—which are great for them to give as gifts. You might also earn a fee for your appearance. Some authors sell thousands of books in this way. Be prepared with an exciting presentation about a theme in your book or your background. Remember, you are an expert about you and your book. A presentation will make for better promotion of your children's book to both students and teachers.

5. DON'T FORGET THE GRANDPARENTS.

According to the Grandparent Economy study by Peter Francese, "In 2009…grandparents will spend $2 trillion. Of this, approximately $52 billion will go toward goods and services for their grandchildren." Offer to talk to local senior groups and senior centres, exhibit your book at local festivals, craft fairs, religious events, and other places drawing families and grandparents.

6. REMEMBER YOUR CAMERA AND ASK FOR TESTIMONIALS.

Everywhere you go, bring your camera, document children reading your book, your presentations, etc., and don't be shy about asking for testimonials. Testimonials from teachers and librarians are especially valuable because they lend credibility to your book. Make sure to include photos, testimonials, appearances, and events on your website and post to your social media.

People are more likely to buy picture books from authors they've met. The more you can speak about your book, the better. Once you have the local area covered and nicely documented on your website, it will give you the base (and experience) to expand your efforts. Future picture book promotions may include reaching out to writers and editors at educational, parenting, grand-parenting, or children's media. Book bloggers and other media outlets can also recommend or help you promote your picture book.

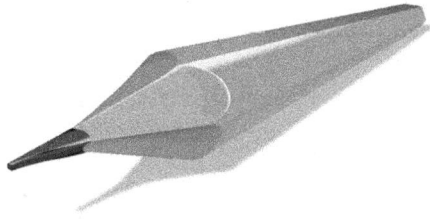

CHAPTER 24

ADAPTATION FOR STAGE AND SCREEN

There is a growing number of stage shows are adapted from picture books. While some authors are content to sell the stage rights to their books and let the theatre company take it from there, others like to have some degree of involvement in the adaptation.

Before you protest your book being adapted to screen, it's important to look at the purpose of these adaptations. While a lot of these adaptations are made for money, these adaptations are made for many other reasons.

Adaptations can ultimately bring a story to a larger audience, expanding the fans of the franchise past just those who love the picture book. To appeal to this larger audience, adaptations must be made to entertain the general public. They can translate your story into a new medium, which can open a lot of opportunities.

Although picture books and theatre have many things in common (see Timothy Knapman's excellent PBD post here), they are very different media and what works well on the page, will not necessarily work well on the stage. Successfully translating a story from one to the other takes a great deal of skill across a wide range of disciplines: the list of creative contributors involved in a stage adaptation may include a scriptwriter, director, composer, lyricist, actors, musicians, set designer, costume designer, puppet maker, and lighting designer. However, in smaller adaptations, individuals will usually take on two or three of these roles.

Here are five things that I've learnt from working with theatre companies on the stage adaptations of my picture books.

✎ 1: DO MAKE A SONG AND DANCE OF IT!

A common ingredient of most picture book adaptations is music and all the shows that have been adapted from my picture books have included songs that were written for the adaptation. Songs are sometimes sung to a pre-recorded accompaniment, but it's not unusual for the music to be played live as part of the performance.

In Belfield and Slater's adaptation of Here Be Monsters all of Simon Slater's score is performed live by a cast of actor-musicians. The original picture book is written in rhyme and Simon incorporated some of the couplets from the original text into his lyrics.

✎ 2. "MAKE 'EM LAUGH!"

Children love to laugh and another common ingredient of many, if not most, picture book adaptations is comedy. In many adaptations the comedy stems from the original picture book, but it's often added into a stage adaptation to provide moments of light relief in more serious stories.

✎ 3. "IT'S GOOD TO TALK!"

Word count restrictions tend to limit the amount of dialogue that authors can include in a picture book. The same restrictions do not apply to stage adaptations and scriptwriters will usually take advantage of this, adding extra dialogue to flesh out characters and embellish the plot.

The Santa Trap's beastly anti-hero Bradley Bartleby spends most of the original picture book alone in his booby-trapped mansion. Consequently, the book has little dialogue and most the story is told in narration (along with Poly Bernatene's wonderfully atmospheric illustrations). Unfortunately, a children's show in which so little is said by the characters is unlikely to hold the interest of a young audience. Belfield and Slater's stage adaptation solved this problem by expanding the roles of the three secretaries who only appear on one page of the picture book. In the stage version, the three secretaries become Bradley's reluctant stooges, giving him someone to talk to (or in Bradley's case - shout at) and interact with throughout the play.

✎ 4. SOMETIMES STORY ELEMENTS HAVE TO BE ADDED IN ...

Entirely original story elements such as new characters, settings, scenes, and subplots are sometimes needed for a stage adaptation.

The original picture book cast of Ruby Flew Too! were joined by two new birdwatcher characters who acted as narrators in Topsy Turvy Theatre's stage adaptation of the book.

✎ 5. ... AND SOMETIMES STORY ELEMENTS HAVE TO BE TAKEN OUT.

The writer's maxim "kill your darlings" applies to adaptations as much as original stories and sometimes much-loved elements of the original picture book need to be removed completely for the story to work well on stage.

A popular element of the original picture book version of The Princess and The Pig is the way characters hold up books they've read to back up their (usually misguided) theories about what is happening in the story. The refrain "It's the sort of thing that happens all the while in books," is repeated throughout the text, culminating in the final punchline, "Unfortunately for the prince, it's not what happens in this particular book". The first draft of Folksy Theatre's script for their stage adaptation of the book retained this refrain and punchline, but it didn't feel quite right for the stage show. Much of the show's audience would be unaware that the story they were watching was adapted from a book, so I felt it would make more sense if the final punchline was altered to, "it's not what happens in this particular story." And once "story" was used in the punchline it had to be swapped in throughout the rest of the play as well. Folksy's scriptwriter and director Lee Hardwicke agreed and cut the "book" references from her script.

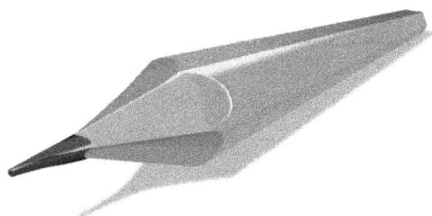

CHAPTER 25

CONCLUSION

L et the wild rumpus begin! Set your dreams of imaginary lands and mythical creatures to life. You've learnt how to inspire a child's imagination by giving them the tools necessary to explore the world around them.

Follow the guides in this course, and you'll craft a beautiful story tailored toward your audience. And you'll have the illustrations to make your children's book eye-catching, and intriguing.

Children value creativity and individuality. There is no one way to draw. No one way to paint. No one way to write. It's about being uniquely you, lending your unique voice to your unique story.

That's why you shouldn't be afraid of the way you write, and you draw because that's what sets you apart. Diversity is important. Tell your story.

www.ingramcontent.com/pod-product-compliance
Lightning Source LLC
Chambersburg PA
CBHW050748030426
42336CB00012B/1716